Triceratops

Contents	Page
Size	2-3
Head and tail	4
Legs and claws	5
Horns	6-7
Fossils	8-9
Hatching eggs	10
Neck shield	11
Beak and teeth	12-13
Fighting enemies	14-15
Name	16

written by Pam Holden

One of the last dinosaurs on Earth was Triceratops. It was an enormous animal that looked like a giant rhinoceros.

It may have lived with lots of other Triceratops in a herd. They were such large animals that they had to go a long way to find enough food.

Triceratops was long, tall, and heavy, with a huge head and a pointed tail.

It walked slowly on four short, strong legs with hard hooves and sharp claws.

The name Triceratops means "three-horned face".

It had one short horn on its nose and two much longer ones pointing forward over its eyes.

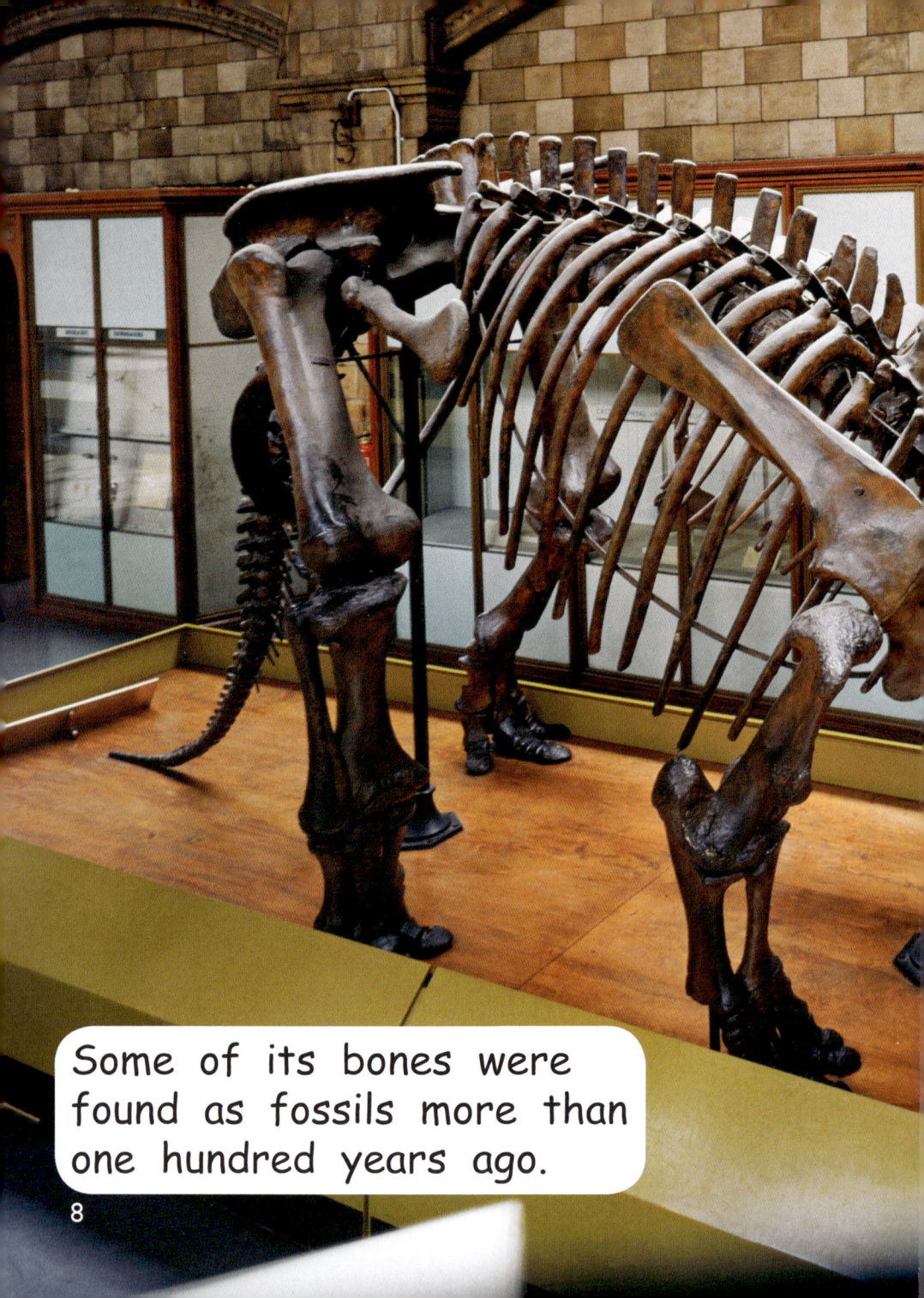

Some of its bones were found as fossils more than one hundred years ago.

Scientists called paleontologists put together horns and claws and teeth. They built a skeleton of Triceratops.

Scientists think that most kinds of dinosaurs laid eggs to hatch their babies. Triceratops grew to be one of the biggest dinosaurs.

It grew and grew until it was about the size of a school bus! It had a large shield around its neck, with a zig-zag of bone at the top.

Triceratops had a sharp beak, like a parrot's beak, at the front of its mouth. There were a lot of sharp teeth, too, for eating plants and leaves. It could have used its long horns to push over trees.

Paleontologists think that Triceratops had to use its long horns to fight off its enemies, like Tyrannasaurus Rex.

They know that T Rex was a fierce and hungry meat-eater that liked to eat other dinosaurs, and their eggs, too.

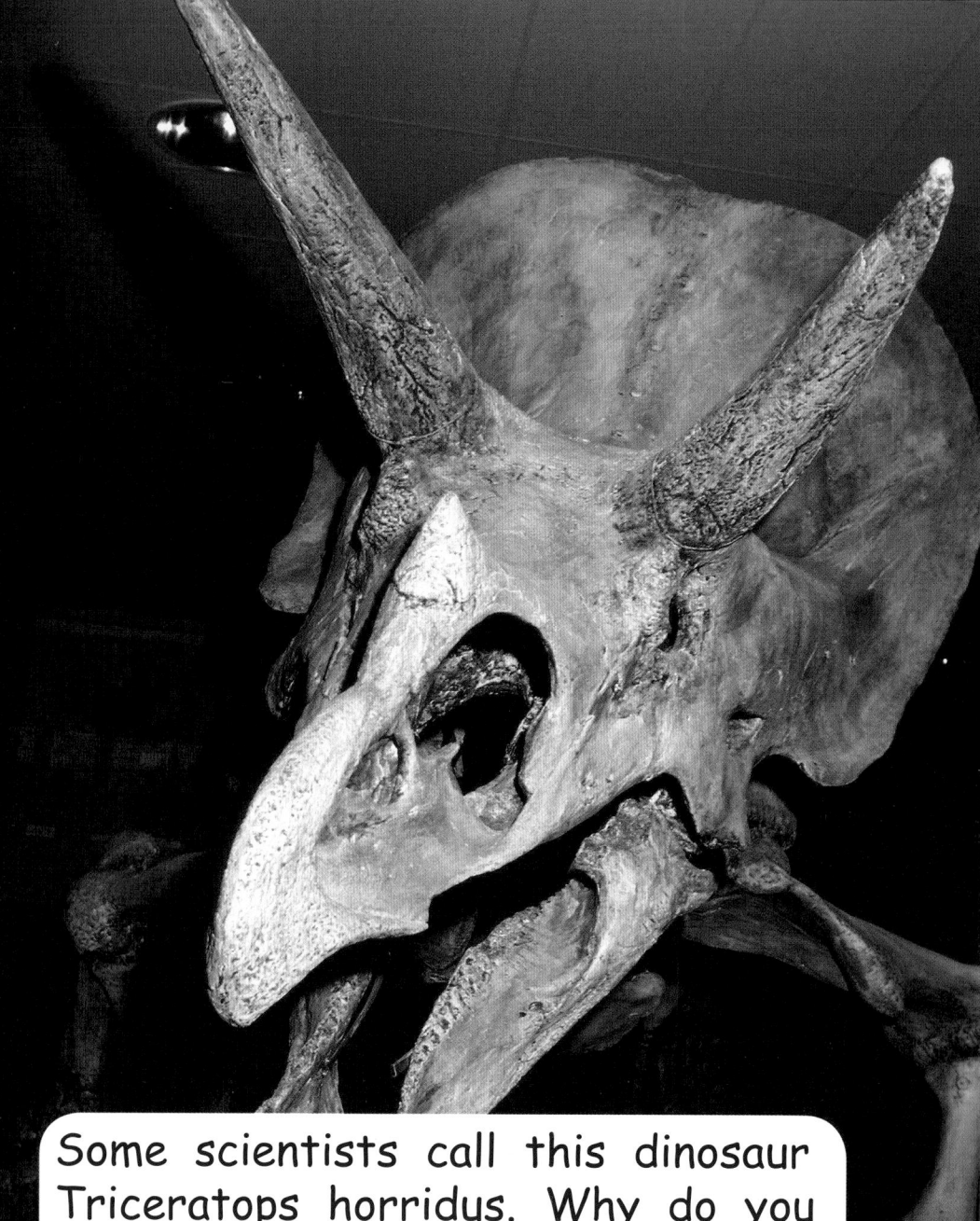

Some scientists call this dinosaur Triceratops horridus. Why do you think they gave it that name?